MESSING

around

ON the

MONKEY

Bars

MESSING around on

and other School Poems

the MONKEY Bars

for TWO VOICES

BETSY FRANCO

illustrated by
JESSIE HARTLAND

CANDLEWICK PRESS

For Tom
B. F.

For my nephew Patrick, who can read a book anywhere—
even upside down on the monkey bars!
J. H.

Text copyright © 2009 by Betsy Franco
Illustrations copyright © 2009 by Jessie Hartland

First edition 2009

Library of Congress Cataloging-in-Publication Data is available.

Library of Congress Catalog Card Number 2008935570

ISBN 978-0-7636-3174-1

SCP 16 15 14 13 12 11
12 11 10 9 8 7 6 5 4 3

Printed in Humen, Dongguan, China

This book was typeset in Avenir.
The illustrations were done in gouache.

Candlewick Press
99 Dover Street
Somerville, Massachusetts 02144

visit us at www.candlewick.com

CONTENTS

AUTHOR'S NOTE

Though these poems can be read silently and enjoyed by a single person, they are the most fun when read aloud by two people.

Voice 1 speaks lines that look like this.

Voice 2 speaks lines that look like this.

Both voices speak lines that look like this, at the same time.

All the poems in this book can be adapted for reading aloud by larger groups. For example, one half of the group can read Voice 1 all together, the other half can read **Voice 2** all together. For some poems, it's more appropriate to have one person read Voice 1, while the rest of the group reads **Voice 2** all together, or vice versa. Jump right in and experiment with your own versions!

Wild Bus Ride

Snort, squeal,
snort, squeal.
We're gobbled up
by a beast with wheels.

Grumble, growl,
grumble, growl.
The beast shoots smoke.
It moans and howls.

Jumble, rumble,
jumble, rumble.
Its big old belly
groans and grumbles.

Screech, cough,
screech, cough.
**It opens its mouth—
we scramble off.**

Snort, squeal,
growl, grumble.
**The beast is gone
with a rumble, rumble.**

New Kid at School

Where did you come from?

Far away.

Miss your friends?

Every day.

Where do you live?

Maple Street.

What's your name?

Call me Pete.

How old are you?

Just turned eight.

You like hoops?

Yeah, great.

Got any friends?

Nope, not yet.

Wanna play?

You bet!

11

Jenny's Pencil

Tap, tap
Tap, tap
Tap, tap
Tap, tap

Tap, tap **While we're reading**
Tap, tap **and we're writing,**
Tap, tap
Tap, tap

Tap, tap **multiplying**
Tap, tap **or dividing,**
Tap, tap
Tap, tap

Tap, tap **Jenny's pencil**
Tap, tap **can't keep quiet.**
Tap, tap
Tap, tap

Tap, tap	**Just today**
Tap, tap	**she caused a riot.**
Tap, tap	
Tap, tap	
Tap, tap	**One by one**
Tap, tap	**we started tapping.**
Tap, tap	
Tap, tap	
Tap, tap	**Soon the class**
Tap, tap	**was really rapping—**
Tap, tap	
Tap, tap	
Tap, tap	**bopping, hopping**
Tap, tap	**snapping, clapping,**
Tap, tap	**drumming, thumping,**
Tappity-tap, tap	**tappity-tapping!**

13

Animal Reports

I might do mine on the great blue whale.
I'm thinking about the valley quail.

Or maybe I'll try the spitting spider.
There's always the yellow-bellied glider.

I might look up the lazy sloth.
My mom said, "Do the luna moth."

I could just pick the leopard seal.
Hey, what about the slimy eel?

Let's get started. What's that say?
"Notes and outlines due
today!"

YIKES!
YOW!
NO WAY!

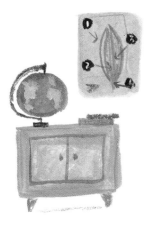

Animal Reports
Notes
and

In the Library

Snicker, snicker
Ouch, eeek
Burp, snort
Tee-hee

Shhh, children.
Time to read.
A quiet room is what we need.

Sniffle, sniffle
A-chooo
Hic-cup
Hee-hee

Silence now,
girls and boys.
Put an end to all your noise.

Pssst, pssst
Giggle, growl
Yip, yelp
Whoopeee!

That's enough!
Listen to me!!
Quiet in the
librar-eee!!!

17

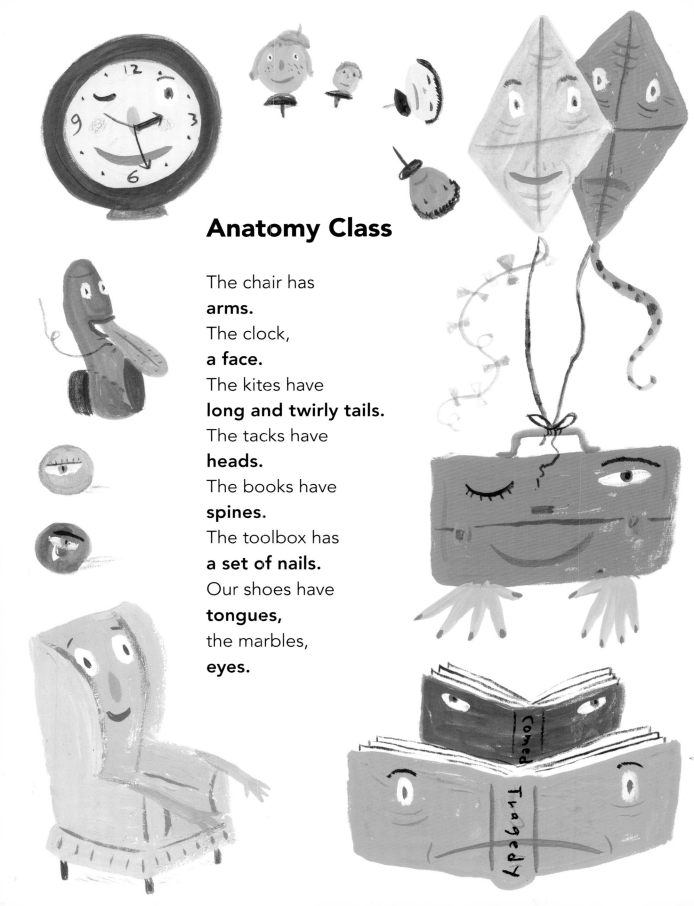

Anatomy Class

The chair has
arms.
The clock,
a face.
The kites have
long and twirly tails.
The tacks have
heads.
The books have
spines.
The toolbox has
a set of nails.
Our shoes have
tongues,
the marbles,
eyes.

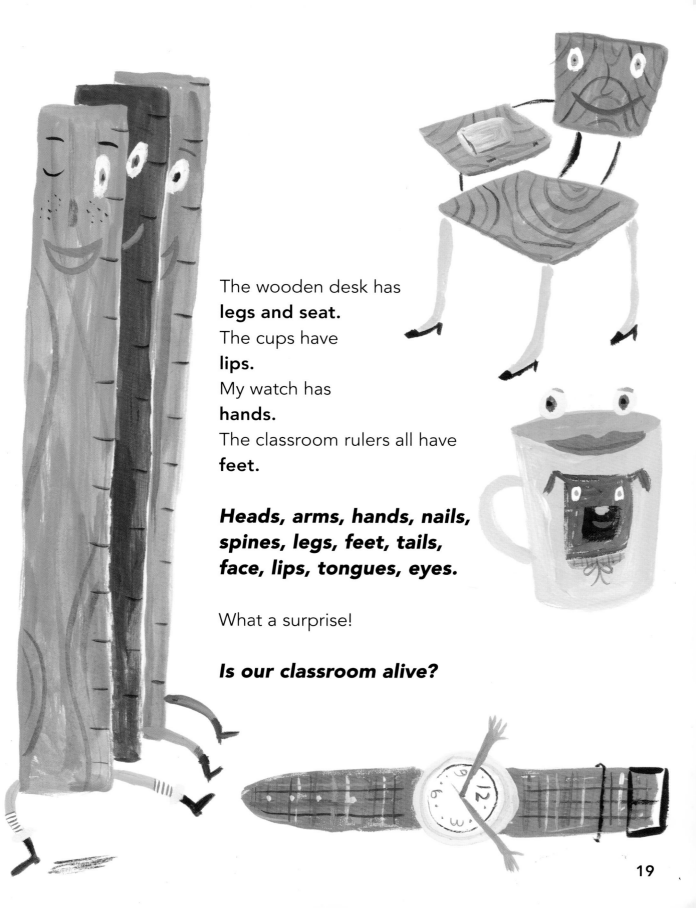

The wooden desk has
legs and seat.
The cups have
lips.
My watch has
hands.
The classroom rulers all have
feet.

Heads, arms, hands, nails,
spines, legs, feet, tails,
face, lips, tongues, eyes.

What a surprise!

Is our classroom alive?

Whirr, Whirr, Zing, Zap

Whirr, whirr.
A spinning fan.
Zing, zap.
A rubber band.
Thud, bonk.
A math book falls.
Boing, boing.
A rubber ball.
Grrr, grrr.
The sharpener.
Vroom, vroom.
The lawn mower.
Rap, rap.
Someone knocks.
Tick-tock.
The classroom clock.

It's tough to do my work today
'cause all the sounds get in the way!

**Whirr, thud, vroom, zap,
grrr, boing, rap, rap.
Sounds in the room
never stop . . .
tick-tock, tick-tock,
tick-tock, tick-tock . . .**

I Can't Wait

Today's the day.
I can't wait.
At recess time,
I won't be late.
I'll meet you by
the mulberry tree.

And then you'll make the trade with me.

I'll trade my little green iguana . . .
for my little sister Donna!

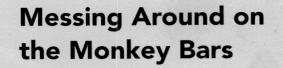

Messing Around on the Monkey Bars

Time for recess!
Here we are,

**messing around
on the monkey bars!**

Hand over hand,
fast or slow,

**calling to
our friends below.**

Skipping two bars,
skipping three,

dangling down
by just our knees.

Swinging up
above the ground,

**missing bars
and tumbling down.**

Hooting, howling,
here we are,

***messing around
on the monkey bars!***

25

Lunch Money

It's lunchtime. Yum!
Quick, get in line.

What's good today?
Can't read the sign.

My money's missing!
Where'd it go?

A hole in my pocket!
Oh, no!

Trays
↓

I'll go and look.
I'll save your spot.

I couldn't find it!
Look what I got.

Two burritos! Way to go!
You're a buddy, don't ya know?

What a pal.
Yeah, lucky I found . . .

a bunch of quarters on the ground.

Jump Rope Jingle

Come on in.
I'll jump with you.
It's double fun
to jump with two.

Jump, jump,
spin around.
Jump, jump,
slap the ground.

Turn to the east.
Turn to the west.
Choose the one
you like the best.

Jump, jump,
A, B,
C.

Jump, jump,
1, 2,
3.

Turn in circles.
Keep the beat.
Feel the rhythm
in your feet!

Backboard Rap

bounce, bounce

bounce, bounce **Dribble, dribble,**

bounce, bounce **Pass to Trish.**

bounce, bounce **Shoot a basket.**

bounce, bounce **Hear the swish!**

bounce, bounce **Dribble, dribble,**

bounce, bounce **Pass to Vin.**

bounce, bounce **Hit the backboard.**

bounce, bounce **Up and in!**

bounce, bounce **Dribble, dribble,**

bounce, bounce **Take a shot!**

bounce, bounce **There's the buzzer.**

bounce, bounce **Yeah! We're hot!**

bounce, bounce

bounce, bounce

bounce

Weird Stuff in the Lost and Found

A purple coat,
a wizard hat,
a dirty baseball shirt,
someone's stinky soccer sock,
a yellow hula skirt.

**They're all mixed up and messy
in a box here on the ground.
My mother begs me every day
to check the Lost and Found.**

Some baseball cards,
a monster mask,
a battered wooden flute,
a frog dressed up in ballet shoes,
a furry winter boot.

They're all mixed up and messy
in a box here on the ground.
My mother begs me every day
to check the Lost and Found.

My yo-yo!
And my squirt gun—
it's mine, without a doubt.

My lunch box filled with garter snakes!
Wow, wait till Mom finds out!

Me and Joe Lining Up After Recess

We race
for the front—

bunch up
and bump,
wiggle,
giggle,
trip,
tease,
push,
pull,
jab,
grab,
poke,
pinch,
squish,
squeeze.

Then Teacher gives the quiet sign,
says,
"You two go to the end of the line!"

35

Back in the Room for the Afternoon

Hey, how do you do, Glue?
I'm all stuck up, and you?

Say, what's the score, Door?
Don't push me around no more.

You got my back, Pack?
Hey, cut me some slack, Jack.

So, what do you say, Clay?
I'm in good shape to play.

See you later, Calculator.
You're my favorite operator!

Homework Blues

Didn't finish your spelling?
Nope.
Can you tell me why?
My brother barfed all over the words.
They're covered with Eskimo pie.

Didn't finish your math?
Nope.
Can you tell me why?
My calculator blew apart!
It looked like the Fourth of July.

Didn't finish your science?
Nope.
Can you tell me why?
A tiny alien stole my work—
right before my eyes.

What a crazy night you had.
Yep.
You must've been horrified.
Yep.
You're staying after school today.
Huh?
Guess the reason why.

Our Tired Teacher Must Not Be Listening

A a B b C c D d E e F f

Can we skip homework? What a bore.
Yeah, okay.
Can we chuck math for tug-of-war?
Yeah, okay.
Can we race skateboards down the hall?
Yeah, okay.
Can we get pizza and go to the mall?
Yeah, okay.
And paint the walls fluorescent green?
Yeah, okay.
And fill the room with jelly beans?
Yeah, okay.

Hooray!

We can skip homework, play a game,
race skateboards, go to the mall, paint the
walls fluorescent green, and stuff ourselves with
jelly beans!

Two Bikes at the Bike Rack

I've seen you rollin' down the street.
Yeah, me too. It's nice to meet.

Look at your lights and all your gear!
I once considered a racing career.

I've got ten speeds. So how 'bout you?
I'm pretty cool with twenty-two!

You don't have scratches, or a dent.
Whenever I crash, I avoid cement.

Hear that *hissss*? You've got a flat.
Whoa, I'd better look at that!

We'll have to talk again sometime.
'Cause here comes Josh.
And here comes Grace.

See ya tomorrow.
Same time, same place.

The Very Best Feeling

There's excited, **delighted,**

scared, **and mad.**

There's happy, **embarrassed,**

surprised, **and sad.**

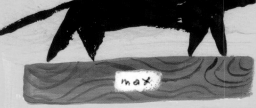

**But the very best feeling
that we've ever had,**

the one that we have every day,

is the feeling we get
when the final bell rings,
and there's nothing to do but just PLAY!

45

ADVENTUROUS WAYS TO READ THE POEMS

Wild Bus Ride (pages 8–9)
Voice 2 could be read by many voices all together. And for a rousing finale, ALL voices can chime in on the last two words in the poem: *rumble, rumble.*

Jenny's Pencil (pages 12–13)
Instead of saying the words *tap, tap,* Voice 1 could tap a pencil on a desktop or a table for a more realistic sound. For more than two readers (and more noise!), two pencils or voices can chime in on the taps for the fifth verse, three pencils or voices on the taps for the sixth verse, four pencils or voices on the seventh verse, and ALL pencils or voices on the last verse. If multiple voices speak the *tap, tap* lines, be sure they are spoken softly so as not to drown out Voice 2!

Whirr, Whirr, Zing, Zap (pages 20–21)
For fun with a large group, one person can read Voice 2 and the rest of the group can divide into eight pairs or eight small groups. Each of those pairs or groups can read one of the sounds assigned to Voice 1. For example, the first pair or group could make the *Whirr, whirr* sound, the second pair or group could make the *Zing, zap* sound, and so on.

Once each pair or group reads its sound, they can continue whispering that sound until the first section of the poem (the first eight lines) is complete. The result will be an "orchestra" of sounds.